RECENT BOOKS

ADMIRAL FEVER (Sailing After Lunch, 1997)

CERULEAN EMBANKMENTS (Living Batch, 1999)

LIGHTS OUT (The Figures, 2003)

FICKLE SONNETS (Fuck A Duck, 2005)

POCKETS OF WHEAT (The Figures, 2007)

REVERSE SPIN : Art Writings (/ubu Editions, 2008)

THE RIOT ACT

GEOFFREY YOUNG

BOOTSTRAP PRESS
2008

Cover painting: "Bathroom Scene #5," 2003, by Eric Fischl

Acknowledgements: Some of these poems were printed
in *Exchange Values Interviews*: Volume 2 (Otolith, 2007);
Likeness (Henry Porter, 2006); *Full Count* (Giggling Fir Trees, 2007);
The Reward (Fershlugginer, 2007); *Shiny;* and *Rough Road Ahead*.
Gertrude Stein provided the lyrics to "Can't Get No Whole One Blues,"
in *The Making of Americans*, p. 521.

Bootstrap Press is an imprint of Bootstrap Productions, Inc.,
a non-profit arts and literary collective founded by
Derek Fenner and Ryan Gallagher.

Bootstrap Productions
82 Wyman Street
Lowell, MA 01852

CONTENTS

WHY I DON'T WRITE NOVELS

I Get Along   11
Cyclops Had An Eye   12
Elemental Forecast   13
The Drop Dead   14
Finally   15
Butterfly   16
I Know You Mean Well   17
The Bane of Western Thinking   18
Why I Don't Write Novels   19
Because of You   20
In A Buddy Grove   21
Linus At The End   22
Of Wetness   23
Trim the Vine   24
I Am Born Again   25
A Syllabus of Swallows   26
Only the Right Word   27
Turning Pages   28
The Fact   29
A Roman Stutter   30
The Leash   31
Sliding Between Houses   32
Mission Chair   33
What Women Want   34
A Single Backyard   35

Graeco Roman Earthlings   36
Down the Garden Pathology   37
The Perfect Shot   38
For Nothing   39
Alone and Aloud   40
Total Victory   41
With What Imprecision   42
Authorizing the Use of Farce   43
Rag Time   44

CONVERSION

The Loon   47
Drying Out   48
No Beethoven in Clouds   49
Flashback   51
The Condition of Presence   53
Late in the Week Police Issued a Description   54
Quantum Foam   55
The Agent   56
According to What   57
Chittlins   59
Bunting in Isla Vista   60
No Single Effort   62
Cleanest   63
Fat Chance   66
Jobless in January   68

Why What?   69
Defender of the Universe   71
X, Y, & Z   72
The Line   74
Bus Stop   76
Program Notes   77

UP THE WAZOO

The Reward   81
Rene Ricard Night At Bill Berkson's Frank O'Hara Talk
    At Poet's House on Spring Street   83
The Madness of Dawn   85
Hail & Farewell   86
Kathleen   87
Heart of the Breath   91
On the Oat Tour   92
Got   94
The 97th Kentucky Derby   95
What's In Store   97
On the Liz Willis Avenue Bridge   98
Up the Wazoo   99
Ron Padgett Reads at Locus Media, 594 Broadway,
    November 30, 2000, 6:30-8:30 PM   102
Can't Get No Whole One Blues   104

WHY I DON'T WRITE NOVELS

For Sharon Gregory

"To me all sonnets say the same thing of no importance."
William Carlos Williams

"And could one make a sonnet of nothing but trees."
Clark Coolidge

"I am not a sonnet, you are not a sea urchin, and this is not
a poetry contest, comrade."
Stephen Rodefer

I GET ALONG

I visit the corner fire to plug in my office
Asking what's Hecuba to me or me to The Doors?
Now I can pee on some trees
And fling this memoir at military brass.

(The Bob in me will do nearly any task.)
Weakness takes root in gullies of the past
But I get along without myself very well.
Does what thinks in me need to know

If "Rain" fell before "Paperback Writer"?
No history of creation can be shelved without twitching.
Hours wear their hats in picture frames.
I'd best use forceps on this wall.

The one Kesey jumped over as an Indian
The one this bubble in the mind calls "foible."

CYCLOPS HAD AN EYE

High on crickets in the dark of discourse
You feel laughably superbad, exposed as any
Flayed Marsyas hiding his pet ogre
Under a shamrock. "Baby Tuckoo, it's bath time!"

Don't tell me. You're a desert mountain peak!
Please scratch your initials on the leather
Cover of the *Rubaiyat*. I understand strata.
My watch-hands atrophied in 1975.

The moon's lazy eye droops for a reason,
Writing degree zero on a cold sore.
The future is over my head
As I shrink to the size of a canyon

A camera on a trackless mount
Scanning for proof that beauty is truth.

ELEMENTAL FORECAST

The film takes place on an island
populated with women and small dogs.
Men have been wiped out by a toxic disaster
along with nearly every species of animal.

Time stands still. The weather is constant and mild.
Trees bear fruit all year long. The women remain
young and nubile, the dogs forever lively and happy.
The women swim and stroke each other while the little

dogs frolic around them. The only sign that men ever
existed is a video of speeches by Arnold Schwartzenegger
which has a soothing effect on the dogs and some women.
There's also a video of "Animal Kingdom," presented by

the Marlboro Man, but no one watches it. It is there
as a testimony to the barbarism of previous eras.

THE DROP-DEAD

I hit "Star Sauce" & catch
The drop-dead to Valhalla
Fizzing like champagne in a hailstorm.
I must ascertain what humans are for

Why we rattle around the glue pots
With hearts gone on alcoholic cake
Our plot lines glowing in the dark.
Even a shined shoe will scuff the floor.

As Salome's comb grooms the Baptist's beard
Straight talk gives friendship a password.
Slip through these vital signs, Tank.
Vampires lose their grip on waffles and syrup.

May no wave of nostalgia fox your paper
No particle of pride trap your music in a piggy bank.

FINALLY

I've had it with font choice, with flush
Left, with fake quatrains. Sibilance
I hereby abjure, onomatopoeia shoo! Die weighty
Enjambment, get thee gone slow syllables, pregnant

Line endings, the whole predictable claptrap
Of stanzaic patterning. Let's embrace
No time's spontaneous mind. Let's calibrate
Sacrifice, criticize power, call a friend

A friend, and live without hogging the harvest.
Tolerance, be the new metric, the "other"
Our erotic porthole. Let's slip into the lap pool,
Get wet with the word, be nothing but brains

Abuzz with irrational bees. Poetry's the coconut
That under the drowned sailor's head finally sprouts.

BUTTERFLY

A low sun
in a platinum haze
with a warm
peeled-peach

tinge
pervading
the upper edge
of a two-

dimensional
dove-gray
cloud, fuses
with the

distant
amorous mist.

I KNOW YOU MEAN WELL

Guido, my son, you need a rest. You're getting
a little loose in the quatrain, if I might say so.
Maybe I can send you bus fare to the Shore
or a couple tickets to Wrestling Tonight?

I don't know. I just want you to be happy
with yourself. You know you take after me.
I got a soft spot in my heart, no matter what
the family says. I know you'll land on your feet

with happy dirt all around. Give your sweetheart
a big hug from Uncle Rootie. And if you need
anything, I'm here for you. They say you been
writing strange poetry. I tell the family, don't

worry, sooner or later he'll get it out of his
system. I know you mean well. God bless you.

THE BANE OF WESTERN THINKING

Tomorrow is a bike, yesterday was flan.
Today's cause and effect
Is delivered by a train
Roaring through a fireplace.

Van Gogh sharpened his quills
On Leonardo's smile, his ink a rush
Of lonely words, his fields
Desperately combustible. How now brown

Bovine? Newton's laws of thermo-dynamics
Are right from a mechanistic
Point of view, but they're lab specific,
Not real world. I need a winning couplet

To say the sonnet is dead. Is there a better
Reason to think this should be read?

WHY I DON'T WRITE NOVELS

A man approaches a closet,
opens the door, reaches in,
selects a shirt, slips it off
the hanger, replaces hanger

on rod, turns from closet
with shirt in hand,
and without shutting closet
door, walks into bathroom,

stands in front of mirror,
puts shirt on, watches
his hands buttoning it, loosens
his belt, tucks shirt into pants,

tightens belt, smiles at
the glass, leaves the room.

BECAUSE OF YOU

A few years ago
I charged into each day
for the game of it,
not sweating the past,

not constructing
a future, but today,
because of you,
I want to drive

to Coney Island
in a light snow,
cross the beach
to the water's edge

and watch the flakes melt
on contact with wet sand.

IN A BUDDY GROVE

Now that we're back on track
The ruts are smoother and William Finn
Sits down to say those early years
In New York when he heard

Someone got an audition
Were devastating
As was asking Richard Foreman to direct
His musical to no avail

But then the right critic said the good thing
In print and life changed from hopeful
To hopped up on the worth
He knew was his at last

Shared by people he cared about,
Wanted to know, and that was that.

LINUS AT THE END

My truck farm is small potatoes
But I am deeply grateful for chickens.
To whisper in her ear is what I think.
Rain has a way with pleonasms.

I can swing a millennial panacea by the tail
And hit your enemy's play-list. But why?
The *omphalos* is a wreath of chili
Attracting moths to your doghouse.

Nobody's happy where they are.
Call me the Darius Painter of palm trees.
Cats sharpen their nails
On the wicker hamper.

Rancor has no place in a glass universe.
Save me the evening of your best day.

OF WETNESS

With crayons,
from memory,
a child is trying
to draw the roiling

heave and swell
of whitecaps
in a passage
of choppy waves

while a parent
at twilight
at the kitchen sink
chops onions

dabbing at
unwanted tears.

TRIM THE VINE

The selfless arugula, the heartless dahlias,
The alien ducks starring in fifteen-second beer spots. . .
Yes the magnificent water glass is my spigot.
We know a wooly mammoth for the stuffing it is

Because the night's still young. Why not "fuggle &
Snuck" at dawn? It takes noble water to float
A cruise, learned clippers to trim the vine.
Drink to me only with thy forehead.

And when furtive labs tempt aging Giants
To marinate their games in juiced swings, would that
Jim Dine's hammer could tap out the melody
To "Well, You Needn't" on their noggins.

Let's settle this hash on an egg or two
Sprinkle our pheromones with cinnamon and sugar.

I AM BORN AGAIN

As from a bridge over Martian poetics
Leaping confutes suspension
And I am born again to guide this noise
Past cat-calls on an inter-stellar runway

Waiting to hear Don Byron's "Spider-Man
Variations" stitch reedy threads
To the moment's crazy quilt.
I need to ramp up my thermal troubadour

Buy chunks of turf to house our mutant brethren.
The marketplace acknowledges no border
Between competing goods. *Mash your tentacles!*
I'm wired to a rectifier shirt that clips folk tales.

When I snarl water smells like bad weather.
A planet shrinks as childhood's street grows stale.

A SYLLABUS OF SWALLOWS

The way this dream house lacks for exits
Is the way diamonds suffer in closed drawers.
No reply, old corridor? I plumb forgot
Your head is a syllabus of swallows, too,

Slow to tape itself to the barn door.
Though you charm my beans with freckled syllables,
Little Orphan, your salt no longer offends
My butter. Plastic like ours was extruded

To bag heroic windfalls. I must go live
In the mustard, drain the woods of every trope,
Find more room to whisper the seasons.
Jars of pickles bleed for Christ in the cellar!

But where's my shovel, holy excavator?
I can dig why trees jockey for light.

ONLY THE RIGHT WORD

I'll tell you what bloke needs a conk
On the Bumstead. Yes you, immortal self!
You shall be known as one who was diddled
By the ideas of salvation and chocolate.

And did you have to insist you were born
The exact minute Rachmaninoff died?
And that you could draw the way a nuthatch
Views a cat? Only the right word walks on water.

When your bike sprints pizza-ward
Its motion scores a tune called "Self-inflicted Type."
Then I hear you singing "Last worthless evening"
Into an ice-cream scoop! Get lost on paper,

McArthur! Too much rock shears the edge
Of a cloud. Too many streets drown in crybaby sake.

TURNING PAGES

Benny "Kid" Paret fluttered
against the ropes
like a titmouse beating his wings in cream
while Emile Griffith the Donatello of the Hotel Champion

pummeled the Kid with smashed potatoes and fireball
jabs, and we leaped off the king-size bed
yelling "Stop it! Stop the fight! He's out on his feet"
to the referee who didn't see it

as Griffith's fists loosened the head
of the Kid from its spinal axis until
finally the leather that was shaping it
could have been fingers turning

pages of a windblown book that
no one will ever read again.

THE FACT

The words in her account of labor and delivery
were as excited and emotional, as painful
and exhilarated, as birth accounts
usually are, even though shortly before

the doctor induced labor she'd been told
her baby was dead. The heroic effort
to push out a nine pound thing, the drama
of sweat and strain—bear down, bear *down*!

what will it be, here it comes, oh he's beautiful—
was said in the forgetting, in the promise,
what she'd been living for, had loved for,
the illusion held for moments until the fact

returned, when with hand reaching, she watched
the lifeless body being taken away, taken where?

A ROMAN STUTTER

There was a time
When I didn't exist
And you didn't exist.
And there'll come a time

When I don't exist
Though you do,
Or a time when
You don't exist

And I do. What
Could be more depressing?
If not to remember
There'll come

A time when
Neither of us does.

THE LEASH

A simple leash
Attached to the neck of a man lying on concrete.
I am holding this leash as I would hold the leash
Of a dog walking Main Street.

I'm wearing fatigues
Tucked into the tops of my boots. You can't see
My breasts under a dark v-neck t-shirt. My hair's
Cropped close. In my left hand is the leash. I look out

At you. The leash is around
My prisoner's neck. He lies naked
On the floor. I have just dragged him into the picture.
I am looking over at him as one of my fellow Americans

Snaps the picture of me and my captive, my dog,
My toy, looking pitiful at the end of the leash.

SLIDING BETWEEN HOUSES

Block this scene with thespian tape
Get looped by something that DJ's do
With mules seen through branches
It's time to sink snot rocks in risible quicksand

Afternoons lay claim to formless things
Sliding between houses like window-washers
Meet the architect of these elevations
Shod in sneakers tied with hyperactive laces

What bubbles inhibit your uniform?
Love's ring-tones sing
"I'll be the knob
Turning inside your locked room"

To catch the shade on decision's blade
To give debt aversion a promising grade

MISSION CHAIR

After lies and torture the feds finally order
Lobster and bubbly for the detainees,
Retooling their bricked-in personalities
With freedom's glaze and lexical radii

As payback for the orange-clad years
Of boredom, sweat and fear. You want
Emergency infusions of allegro juice? You got it.
Justice at last, country-less integers?

Persist, oh captured hard luck cases.
I bow before the cult of your resistance,
Its mission chair. Loose lips install chips.
Bill me for sorcery at the tree factory, Hill.

Historians who dig for truth in Harmsville
Must first breathe the stench of Living Death.

WHAT WOMEN WANT

I engorge this poem to feed an orchestra
Impromptu seeds moistened with source code.
I swear the universe rings like a cash register
When I see your hair go cellular

And your earrings swing like distant oil
Derricks. That's when your name is broken into
Like sonic matter floating on global tides.
There is nothing left to do but grind it up.

Aliens can live on oxygen, too.
Makeover moments delay the dinner bell
Before guests take their seats at The Human Race.
May your favorite philosopher be sensitive

To what women want from bulbs
Stored in cellars. Outrageous blooms.

A SINGLE BACKYARD

We the undersigned
glow in the dark
like children in parks
playing with holes

imagine huge logs
balanced on Niagara's precocious lip.
The kettle hisses, steam
burns. Leaf-peepers

on a family drive ask
what does a single backyard owe us?
When do our parents really die?
Any back spasm tells it true,

soldier. Poetry removes the world.
We stay young forever.

GRAECO ROMAN EARTHLINGS

If this planet is home
If we are truly the observer
And the observed
It is because we were

Produced by the physics here.
Plus ça change
Plus c'est le même texte.
But the real legacy

Of these last few months is Molly Bloom
Writing the lost lines
Of Archilochus.
We're endorsing *Lysistratus* as state policy, FYI.

Call me Red Poppies,
The Delphic monk of bees.

DOWN THE GARDEN PATHOLOGY

After great pain a formal
invitation comes to return
to the sidewalks of daily life.
Dishes in the sink await our love

of *verismo* as fruit flies
await their apotheosis in garbage.
Share-croppers played checkers
with bottle caps; will our unborn

grand-children know orthodontia?
Our islands sink below the reach of satellite?
Each child of privilege shall hold
her guts in hunger, the way

a parking lot looks after rain,
The way they say you lose everything to gain.

THE PERFECT SHOT

Dipping a bucket
Into the sludge of the unconscious
You come up with enough
Dreck to move the poem

From one image
To the next contiguity disorder
After which you try "to hang"
Its skeletal structure

On a clothes-line of semantic beats,
The mind providing a drum.
The bucket's the same one you held
As a child, in a sandbox, a parent

Watching, camera in hand, eager to stop time,
If only for a moment, with the perfect shot.

FOR NOTHING

I shudder like a Victorian with broken stairs
scraping paint from artless moments
to gut the past. Or should I splash
the present with vitamin water

to tell Love's bawdy tale?
Loose suns play havoc with future shacks.
Professor Toolbelt asks for nothing
but asphalt shingles and pointed brick

to feel like Superman in work clothes
doing *xi-gong* with Chinese women.
Think fast, *mes enfants*, when bronc-riding a scud.
We can only patch plaster with dry echoes.

Escape may be gentler with a notebook,
emotion settling like leaves in a washout.

ALONE AND ALOUD

In the gloom
beyond the proscenium
of the blinding
desk-lamp

a politburo of
scornful censors
eavesdrops on
each uttered thought

knowing full well
writing gives voice
to hectic meditation
scuffling alone

and aloud to itself,
to liberate you, dear freedom.

TOTAL VICTORY

Not for another
Minute will I sit here
On my thumbs
And listen to this grommet

Pitch symbolic tomatoes
At the quagmire
Of Baghdad.
I'm for total

Victory, which means
Dragging this fool into
The chambers of the World Court
To be tried, convicted

And sentenced for invasion,
Murder, & monstrous mayhem.

WITH WHAT IMPRECISION

Let us now praise famous waves
Noticing with what imprecision
A hard wind blows spume off crests
Like the one on which the Lone *Etranger* shoots

The curl wearing knee-length spandex tights
While a soldier two reels ahead in a different flick
Reads a "Dear John" letter in a jungle motor-pool
The footage edited to showcase Betty Boop

Back home in "Sorry Fred, America"
Could be any Betty named Jane with a shark tooth on a chain
Lonely as a butter pat melting on a tired plot
Love's crimes fill this cup with Rhone wine

Like a desert our images live after us as dust
Picturing "your name here" impaled on cactus

AUTHORIZING THE USE OF FARCE

The President says, "The public knows
The difference between politics and reality."
Based on what, lies? Slimy distortions? Hidden agendas?
We're winning! No. The logos is so hot its dog tags

Are melting. We're in the triple-bypass heart of no country.
We're fishing the Euphrates where men lose semen.
There are nothing but hotels for us rockers to trash.
No speech on this river can escape the heat.

True narrative pours the drinks and they flee from me.
Soldiers in body bags don't know they've landed.
Late at night, lonely as a child, listening through walls.
Noise spreads war over diplomatic failure.

A bad feeling constricts us with impotent rage.
This page can't be read too closely.

RAG TIME

The name is Keyless Entry. I lecture
On Spanish olives. Tie a lamb chop around my neck
I'll draft you a Byronic stanza, I'll feed
George Herbert's IQ to Liverpool quarrymen.

I must hover over your patio brick,
Peep with this pen to tune your grand piano.
Jakob wrestled with an angel on Bob Dylan's
Beach towel, because snakes have two penises,

As Einstein was quick to point out. You can't take
A warehouse out for steak. Leave the Vermeer
Chair empty, Porgy. For the finale, we'll play
"Krakens on Crackers," and remember to smile.

Nobody loses sleep like fiends of the backbeat.
If you don't carry stamps you're not a poet.

CONVERSION

For my brothers Laf and Bo

"I couldn't see her face, so I painted the make-up."

Alex Katz

THE LOON

ALL HE WANTED WAS THIS: to sit, look out a window, and write.

"This world is too horrible for words," he typed, a juvenile truism across the top of the screen.

"The reason I'm messed up is, I was born with an identical twin who died when he was a day old, and sometimes I think I'm him."

"I can determine someone's intelligence by the direction their feet point as they walk down the street."

"Without sails or wings, I fly through the night, just above the snow, around each tree in the forest, by moonlight. OK, what am I?"

"The wetlands are gray. We are plagued by doubt. Yet we accept, with an almost reverential holiness, the deadening rituals of the day to day."

"A ghost is that part of your feeling you don't feel."

"Talking, before hand, about sex, is a kind of sex."

"Only a few could be reached by the little bell."

"Engulfed by the power of love, he fell right in."

"Pain is my anesthetic."

"What I have said in my poor fashion, I have said."

"You don't stop to think of the rough places after the road is made."

DRYING OUT

YOU GOT UP AND SHAVED. After smoking a cigarette, you went back to sleep, only to get up an hour later and shave again. Then you returned to bed.

Another hour later you woke. You walked into the bathroom, drew water in the sink, got out your razor, shaving mug and brush before we stopped you.

"You've shaved twice already this morning," we said.

With the weariness of Lazarus you asked if we were kidding.

"No, it's true, feel your chin. Two times this morning already, and this makes three."

You stood there uneasily, your memory struggling in quick sand, trying to wake up, trying to wake up twice.

We walked you back to bed, sat with you in silence, then told you you'd feel more like getting up tomorrow. And left you there, rubbing your chin, not a whisker on your face.

NO BEETHOVEN IN CLOUDS

SHE WAS NOT IN THE CEREAL. She was not in the sound of the plastic lid being removed from the yogurt. She was not in the freckles on the banana-skin, nor in the slice, nor the knife. There was a little bit of her in the blue canister of brown sugar, in the spoon with a wooden handle, in the long ago memory of when they were new. But of the milk, what can be said? She was not in the milk. Of mooing there was none.

Strange house, mantled around their shoulders, with tiny snowflakes criss-crossing at the kitchen window. Speech was just adequate to them, they were so white, and so few.

She was in the cup, however, coffee sitting hot on cool table-top. She was in the cigarette, the lighter, the ashtray. Tiny flecks of light in her eye reflected the snow in the yard. Winter had arrived, the heat kicked on, hot air rumbling under the floorboards as under a shirt when the motor of the heart hurts.

They filled their cups again and got to work, each typing, each sorting, each de-corporealizing, each lost to the other.

How to unblock the channels, patch the frayed cuffs, amend the document? What finally was the point.

The cat leapt on the table to lap the milk left in their bowls.

There is no urn worthy of holding the dust on this desk. No stomach able to digest each camouflaged word.

There were oranges in a bowl, but no Beethoven in clouds.

With a kiss the lover transforms the loved one, takes possession in mind. But later, perhaps in a split second, the nicknames of a decade of life lived are rejected, appointments unravel, genes collapse on inert chromosomes. Later, she will not be there. Later, the toy that was love will rust. Later, a street will disappear in a mudslide. Later, each phrase will fly by, ungrasped.

FLASHBACK

IT'S MID-JANUARY, THE 16th, to be precise, I'm on Downing Street, on Bedford, on Carmine, I'm the vernacular pouring across W. Houston and 6th when a hurtling cab makes me leap to safety over a patch of last week's snow. As my expletive dissolves in air, I pass an empty bench next to a metal trash can, the same heavy trash can from a few summers ago, and in a flash the story comes back to me.

I'd just flown in from the Coast. It was summertime in the Village. I was out walking after midnight when some white guys in a van stopped at Bleecker and 6th, jumped out like shock troops leaving their van door open and ran yelling at a few winos asleep on the benches. As the winos wake and scatter, one guy gets isolated, and the white guys are on him. The wino back-pedals, staggers, dodging insults and fists—he's barely fending them off—when a metal trash can flies through the air, hits the wino in the head, the can banging to the cement and rolling to a stop in the gutter.

This is the split second, the why god moment. Hush little baby don't you cry. Out of nowhere they'd arrived, attacked, and once they saw the blood spurting, had backed off. And in that brief interval the black man spotted me, standing behind him, his hand pressed to his forehead to try and stem the flow.

I say, "This way," motioning down Downing and a possible exit from the action, but I'm white too, he does a double take, the vigilante thugs get back in their van and split on tires screeching

51

like the movies. Blood is gushing from the man's forehead, his filthy t-shirt is bright red, we make it down Downing to Varick, I hail a cab, I hail a lot of cabs, but every cab that almost stops sees a blood-spattered black man, it's almost two in the morning, they peel out with a disgusted wave of their hands.

Bessie!

After painful minutes, a young black cabbie stops, he's wearing dark-rimmed glasses, I say, "You and I don't take this brother to St. Vincent's right now he's a dead man."

He looks at the blood, looks back at me, says, "Get in."

Ten blocks later we're there, we thank the driver, we're in the emergency waiting room, walk up to the window, lots of people around, other stories, collapsing bodies, nurses in white shoes, paper to be filled out and I say, "This guy's been bleeding for an hour, there's no time for filling out forms," and the nurse turns to him and asks, "You gonna faint?"

Man says "Yes," and as she wheels up a chair and sits him down in it, he winks at me, and smiles, he must be in shock or still numb from grape, or both, but the wink means I ain't gonna faint, and yes I'll take the treatment no bullshit delays.

As she wheels him directly into Emergency he's saying, "Stay with me, what's your name, come with me, let's talk." But I wave so long, don't get his name, don't give him mine, say good luck, shoot him a smile, turn, and duck out the hospital door.

THE CONDITION OF PRESENCE

GUS RISES AT DAWN, brews a pot of tea, walks to the weight room in the basement where with Biblical intensity he revisits key paragraphs in Western Philosophy.

His brain burns with commentary. He scratches notes to himself on foolscap. Can you really know that you don't know? Separate subjective and objective? Where does it go when the feeling for the poem disappears?

Gus throws the *I Ching* on the bed, mumbles a few words under his breath, then flattens his stomach with a hand, trying to decide between Mexican and Indonesian.

Would a hot meal change his bilious scowl to happy chat? Should he walk into town and window-shop for old sheet music?

The dream hangs over his head; will he reach for it anyway? Every decade a new theme emerges, before the last one has been fully explored.

Meanwhile, botched Ad campaigns yield to the advances of a Korean competitor, and huge corporate settlements are welcomed in the press, etc. Time, he could see now, was on its own side, only. Supremely indifferent.

He knows it is bad for the amplifier to be left on all day. He sees months of paper piling up on his desk. He wonders how much exercise his heart gets when he fulminates.

Drawing primitive faces with a cane in desert sand. . .

"The Shape of Jazz to Come" would be his funeral music. He played it again and again.

"Leave your mark," he wrote. "Leave it right out on the lawn for all to see."

LATE IN THE WEEK POLICE ISSUED
A DESCRIPTION

SUNLIGHT STREAMED THROUGH the stained glass windows of the
Prime Minister's office. For the first time Margaret Thatcher
let herself feel how close she'd come to death at the hands of the
Irish Republican Army.

"It just occurred to me that this was a day I was not meant
to see," she told reporters.

Hidden behind a panel in the bathroom of a 7th floor hotel
room were twenty pounds of Frangex, a brand of gelignite made
only in the Republic of Ireland. It had been planted days or
even weeks before Thatcher and her government arrived for the
annual Conservative Party Conference. Sorting through the
rubble of her feelings, the incident raised questions she strug-
gled to answer.

The chance of finding any meaningful clues grew slim. A
thin man, about 35, brown hair, a mustache and beard that
came down to his chest: how could this help? The London
stock market took its steepest dive in history, the cut in crude
signaling a drop in British revenues, the pound declining against
increasingly expensive imports, coal miners still out on strike.

A thin bearded man could change his appearance in a trice.

As rain soaked the tons of shattered masonry, Thatcher con-
fronted a very cold, a very political winter.

"You could not have endured it, " she said.

QUANTUM FOAM

PARIS, A PUSHPIN HOLDING a cosmic wormhole in place, is a shortcut between centuries linking Caesar to Poussin, connecting Quasimodo to Jarry's squat apartment on the Rue Cassette, exposing Nadar's chemicals to Denis Roche's cigarettes.

Now a mobylette slices through traffic that Pissaro will never paint again. A bus turns down la Rue de Rennes amidst fumes that Stein will never breathe again. The classical world is nothing but causality stocking enigmas on high shelves.

If the poem is scissors, the voice paper, and time the rock. . .

Let's pick our way past Rodin's statue of Balzac, where late night communication transpires between a young ex-pat and Honoré himself, the all-night taxonomist.

"Throw back your less than majestic shoulders," the author of *The Human Comedy* seems to say, "and cross your arms like mine. Lift your chin's stubble a feverish iota and stare into the hard life of the street. Then write all night in a white robe."

The young man says "Thank you, Maestro," still looking up at his companion's heroic pose, "and goodnight," before walking a block to his apartment on la Rue Bréa.

Rain shines on the paving stones. Decades kick through dust.

The novel of the moment? Laura's belly miming the French curve.

The cup is in her hand, hot for a moment only. The tea is real.

THE AGENT

I WAS ALREADY FUNCTIONING as an agent, already putting people and their products together with other people and their products. Once united, these people and their products began to benefit. But I wasn't benefiting. No, I wasn't. My intuition, my skills—what I came to think of as my god-given talent—we were not being seated at the table when the pie was cut up.

So I enrolled in Agent School. Actually it was just a course offered at the local college. After writing my thesis, "On Taking Charge: The Art of Compromise," I had a business card printed up with my name and phone number. I started advertising in a select group of leading literary magazines, and one thing led to another—this was all a decade ago—and now I represent the 145 leading American novelists and story writers, am too busy even to socialize with them, hardly have time to glance at their work, wish I could scale back, but you know, we're one big family, you should see my desk, I feel they need me.

ACCORDING TO WHAT

LEWIS SAT DOWN, SIPPED the Chablis, and asked us if we'd seen Viva.
No, we hadn't seen Viva, nor had we seen Jasper Johns, either, even
though it was his opening. Was there a connection? Later when
I did see Viva standing in the middle of the auditorium wearing
a brilliant green knee-length evening dress talking with her com-
panion Walter Hopps whose face hadn't changed in the five years
since last we'd discussed Guy Williams, I walked up to her kissing
miles of celluloid memory to let her know how nearly fatal to my
academic career the viewing of *Nude Restaurant* and *Lonesome Cow-
boys* had been back in 1970. This lavish praise and rather frontal
presentation of the case caused her eyes to roll into my face, as it
were, in a spiral fashion I felt yielded some otherwise hidden mean-
ing regarding the nature of chemicals. Her nose, it was clear, was
almost touching mine, and her head tilted about twenty degrees off
of its normal vertical axis. She looked wonderful. And to think
that Lewis never did find her seems a shame. Because, when I told
Viva that he was looking for her she said, "Oh where is Lewis?"

I had forgotten about Viva in the years since she starred in films.
But now in her presence I realized how much I missed the autobio-
graphical documentation in time that film preserves of its stars. And
did she miss the coverage? No, I answered myself. Would *Lonesome
Cowboys* still seem outrageously wasted today? Yes, I guessed.

I chanced a tactless remark about her French husband, it being
apparent he wasn't here, and Walter (bless him), cut in with, "He's
back in Paris sucking butt." Lightly he gave Viva a peck on the lips
and shared a sip of his drink with her. Then a woman came up to
Walter with one of those socialite moves, tugging him away with
"Walter may we have you for just thirty seconds?"

I stood alone with Viva in her green dress. I wanted her to tell me something profound about her life in one momentous and intimate verbal rush, just as I wanted to tell her something about mine, but questions and answers seemed senseless, amidst the steady buzzing hubbub of a museum opening. Her daughter was seven years old now.

I swallowed the Chablis. Viva's red hair was drawn back over her ears. We stood there, looking around. Clearly there were no Jasper Johns paintings hanging in this room, because the one picture that caught our eye did so with its witless, inert, and embarrassing shapelessness, otherwise noticeable as a blue blob floating blandly over a deliberate blurt of pea-green. We seemed to see it at the same time.

"That's an unforgivable piece of shit up there," she gestured.

"I couldn't agree more," I said.

(OCTOBER 20, 1978)

CHITTLINS

I DON'T CARE HOW MUCH soul you've got, Ernie. This house smells worse than a bedridden anchovy. The tourist office of my head's nausea center is wobbling like a seahorse in ether. Your chittlins are trying to crawl out from under the ketchup! Even my plate is staring back at me, like a severed head, horrified.

You ask, do I like them?

Oh man.

Praise be to Marvin Gaye singing "What's Goin On" in the background. And thanks for inviting us to watch the game on TV.

Hospitality is always appreciated, brother.

But pass me the corn bread.

BUNTING IN ISLA VISTA

I WAS A GRAD STUDENT in 1967 when Basil Bunting, then 67, came to teach at our school. It was Hugh Kenner, the author of *The Pound Era*, who had invited the poet to Santa Barbara. At the time Bunting suffered from bad eyesight, his thick lenses evidence of complications from cataracts, glaucoma, or worse, for which he underwent several operations.

Bunting taught a class called "Yeats Pound Eliot." His preferred method of teaching was to read aloud from *The Cantos*, from Eliot's *Four Quartets*, and from anything by Yeats. Bunting was absolutely convinced that good poetry didn't need criticism; good poetry needed sounding. Aloud was the way the music of the poetry lived, in the breath and pulse of the reader's voice.

Day one he read Pound's first five Cantos, relishing their vowels, rhythms, and sonority with a voice we could only think of as Bardic, hearing for the first time Bunting's great rolling Northumberland R. He said it was unnecessary to track down all the references, unless inclined to. A serious reader, or someone grooming himself to be a scholar, would naturally do a little digging. To test us, we didn't write critical essays, we just had to be able to identify isolated individual lines from various poems, by author. Was this line by Yeats, Pound or Eliot? Indicate by putting a Y, a P, or an E next to the line.

If you'd read the poems and weren't deaf to particular vocabularies and syntactic idiosyncrasies, it was easy to choose the right poet, even if you hadn't read that exact line before.

Once at the college art gallery I saw Bunting standing a mere two inches in front of the surface of an old drawing, moving his eyes slowly over its lines and volumes. Now I realize it wasn't just a function of his limited eyesight that drew him to the surface, too close to see the actual image as a whole, but that he wanted to see as intimately as possible the hand of the artist, the hand whose line was crucial and whose composition was the result of innumerable decisions in the movement of the line. Was that line efficient, nervous, frivolous, essential? Did it serve the subject matter, or merely delight in its own virtuosity?

Often, on campus, we'd see Maria, his dark-haired sixteen-year old daughter. Bunting told us it gave him untold pleasure to hear her break out laughing as she was reading *Ulysses*.

One day we dropped in on him in his modest little apartment in Isla Vista, an apartment no different than a thousand other cheap little beach-town student apartments, with a Formica table in the kitchen and a few crummy chairs. He was alone. He had just awakened from an afternoon nap, had brewed a pot of coffee, and with knife in hand, was about to spread honey on a few pieces of toast.

We sat down and watched the knife in Bunting's hand as carefully he put honey on the bread, one bite at a time. We watched him chew and we watched him swallow. We watched him sip from the cup of black coffee. Then, with paper napkin in hand, we watched him wipe a glistening teardrop of honey from the bristles of his mustache, the author of "Briggflatts," "Villon," and "Chomei at Toyama," as we talked about who knows what, in this little surfboard town, thirty years ago.

NO SINGLE EFFORT

NO SINGLE EFFORT CAPTURES the essence of the human condition. But the completion of any day's writing adds its particular brush with experience to the master list of competing versions, even if no one reads it for a thousand years.

Why?

Because the time is ripe. We are still green. I look in vain for adults. Nothing but kids on this watch. Six or seven feet tall. Hard to discipline. A good sign in growing boys? Tell me a myth I haven't heard.

The lake of the mind stores wetness. Drying up is our worst enemy. For a person in my shorts I can imagine nothing worse.

It takes a meadowlark in a field. It takes a futon in a loft.

How much time do we have. How much face. You know more than I do. Three chords worth. I've never seen such music.

Call it a self-knockout.

Will Prospero set us free?

A black line traps the image. We suffer people too much. Grainy landscape with noon train. Roll the credits.

CLEANEST

Voici l'histoire, though I'd rather be telling you in a cafe or bar. Maybe it was twenty minutes before the start of the concert. I went downstairs to find the men's room, walked along a corridor (the concert was at Williams College, early 1984), when suddenly I became aware of the sound of a saxophone warming up, then knew, of course, it had to be Garth Hudson, and that The Band were down here, in one room or another, killing time before they had to go on.

I turned into the men's room, one sink, one urinal, and one toilet. I stood at the urinal, listening to the sound of the toilet flushing in the stall to my right. Men know vulnerable, as with back unprotected, I felt the man come out of the toilet and pass behind me over to the sink, where he started washing his hands. Ever the empiricist, I remember not smelling anything.

Glancing to my left, I saw the loose unkempt curls of a brown-haired man, bending a little at the waist, beginning to soap his fingers, the hot water continuously running. It was Richard Manuel, hollow-cheeked piano man, and sometime singer, sometime drummer. I asked him if he was going to sing "Georgia On My Mind" tonight, he being the only white guy I'd ever heard risk it after Ray Charles' version.

"None of the guys seem to know it anymore," he said.

Manuel busied himself with a thorough, steady soaping, then rinsed off. I zipped up, then told him how much we loved The Band's great group sound, and that I'd been in San Francisco back in April of 1969, that first night at Winterland when The Band finally went public, the night that Robbie had to be hypnotized to go on stage he was so frightened.

Richard didn't move for a second, then he started to soap his hands again, saying, "Yeah, that was rough. We had to keep Robbie going with our eyes."

With great concentration Richard finished lathering. I stood to the side of him now, watching him move his hands into the flow of the hot water.

"Who sings on 'It Makes No Difference,'" I asked him, because in that sifty group sound, where a contrapuntal heave made their close harmony so muscular with emotion, I couldn't always be sure who was singing lead.

"That's Rick Danko," he answered.

"Great song," I added.

But Richard stayed bent over at the sink, started lathering his hands again, this for the third time.

"I'd love to hear you sing 'Lonesome Susie' tonight."

Richard looked up, flashed a quick smile, and said, "So would I."

I repressed a huge desire to sing the line "Anyone who's felt that bad, could tell me what to say." I was just standing there, I had no further business in the restroom, and I was getting worried about the soap, the hot water, his endless lathering.

In farewell I said, "Enjoyed talking. Have fun up there tonight."

He looked over, made eye contact, and said, "Same," dipping his head politely, then returned to his hands.

I walked back to my seat feeling horrible, feeling heartsick, but at the same time excited, as if suddenly I were privy to some dark secret so compelling in its insistence that soon I would be telling Clark and Susan all about it.

A year later we read in the newspaper that Richard Manuel had been found dead in a Florida motel bathroom, a suicide by hanging.

FAT CHANCE

TOLD MYSELF TO STAY IN, eat right, proof *The Crystal Text*, then log eight in the rack so that I'd be strong and quick and concentrated the next morning on the tennis court, but no. Instead, I meet up with you, the secret you of bi-coastal trysts, on Fifth Avenue at a party for an English mystery writer. Was she your second cousin? We hadn't read her books.

Five years later I can still recall the ice in the glass, bodies arrayed on sofa and chairs, but no faces. Her publishing house kept this apartment for visiting writers. A former animal with white fur topped the pile of coats in the bedroom. We stayed, talked some, got a little drunk listening to Alexander Cockburn and his brother Andrew exchange political quips. I remember one of the Cockburns chatting you up, and thinking you could be his brother, same fair skin and hair. Then we left, out into the cold, walking twenty windy blocks down 5th Avenue on dirty snow to the Plaza Hotel, feeling giddy and numb in the anonymous cold.

We managed a few winks before dawn, sleeping in Annabel's place on Mott, but woke hung-over, irritable. You were frustrated that you hadn't come. Why did we always drink so much, you asked. You thought perhaps you had somehow failed our friendship, even as I was thinking that maybe it was my fault. Awkward morning where you had to be somewhere, I had to be somewhere else. We couldn't seem to make our plans fit.

It had been a few years since your marriage ended, and I knew you were looking. I was just then exiled in New York, sorting out the echoes of my own evaporating vows. But as much as we seemed to share, you were too ready for a future, I was too mired in a past. Your hope was that we could meet again later so that you could give me your orgasm as I'd given you mine, tenderly held and fiercely felt.

Letting you out the kitchen door into the dingy hallway, you turned once and looked back, both of us alone, in need, no longer in a place, but in between, you wondering if I was perhaps the one, while I, disgusted with myself for having drunk too much and slept too little, felt dumb.

I got my equipment together then, drank another glass of water, and headed out into late morning air, suddenly eager to lose myself in the pleasure of friendly combat with a player whose game plan would be impossible to ignore, just as the sexual uncertainty of the space between us was becoming less than necessary to fill. It would be there when . . .

JOBLESS IN JANUARY

SEVEN GUYS WEARING BLACK gloves toss a leather football around the asphalt playground at the corner of West Houston and 6th on a Thursday morning, no national holiday, just young men throwing the ball around, which is what I'd like to be doing. But I don't cross the street and join them for a few down and out thirty yard strikes in my clumpy work boots and parka, though it's tempting.

I understand what they're doing and why they're there, and especially why one guy not particularly tall or strong makes a leaping catch then breaks away with the ball, holding it extended in one hand like Dr. J driving to a nearby hoop only to miss by a hair or two a stylishly considered dunk.

WHY WHAT?

Resolution

Staring with contempt at a fading photograph of Yosemite granite hanging on the wall of the doctor's waiting room, the sick man said, "I'm going to beat this disease just to do a painting for this office."

Thomas

A week before the end, standing by the foot of his bed, frail with cancer and painkillers, the sick man points to his hand and says, "Thomas." Then to his elbow and says, "Thomas." Raising his eyes slowly to his shoulder the old man says, again, "Thomas," at which point the sick man's friend reaches over and removes an ant from the sick man's upper arm. Looking up at his friend, the sick man says, "Thomas."

Why What?

Midnight, asleep, the sick man's radio is on low, a glass of water within reach next to a pack of Camels.

My alarm's set for three, to deal him his next pill. I've just finished Ford's *Some Do Not*, with *No More Parades* up next, holding myself aloof from hope, able to acknowledge a morbid fascination with death's stealthy approach. Then I remember how surprised I was this morning to see an old lady in front of the house, leaning against the gray trunk of a Queen palm. Too weak to walk further, she was taking a breather, the corner store still half a block away.

As if to the skin of the tree, or to some invisible hand, or eye, she kept muttering, in a tiny voice, "Why, why?" followed by "Why, why?" Was she about to faint, did she need a ride?

Concerned, I approached, asking my curious and not unsympathetic question, "Why what?"

And without missing a beat, or really seeing me at all, she said, in a timorous, quavering voice, "Yes, why what?"

DEFENDER OF THE UNIVERSE

SUDDENLY THERE'S A TERRIBLE agitation as Voltron is backed to the wall. But you and I are sitting together, so what do we care if the sound hurts our ears, the chase scenes extend forever? We've already sliced the onion, crushed the garlic, grated the carrot and diced the bell pepper, tossing it all into a bubbling sauce.

And we've opened the mail to find two book orders for five books, so now we'll cash the checks, buy a cheap pot to boil the noodles in, and pick up a cheese-grater while we're at it. Dinner's at six. And you, my fine-feathered offspring six years old, will be right by my side, a bike-riding tyro eager to make the next major item on the list even if it's only a stop at the post-office to mail the aforementioned books.

An overcast sky provides even light as we cut through parking lots and wheel down streets, saying, "First one to that tree," or "Beat you to the bank," while singing "All I need is a miracle, all I need is you."

"Defend" is what we're going to have to do for ourselves anyway as these trumpeted explosions and staggered ricochets of the cartoon kingdom draw us deeper into the infamy of a universe of brightly lit robots and nefarious zombie giants quick to thwart our passage through space. We've got the little deck-of-cards-size remote gizmo of our first color TV in hand. We're feeling kinda average now, happy to play dumb, watching good beat evil, and evil beat good.

X, Y, & Z

SHE WAS BORED. She hadn't heard a good story in ages.

So that night he offered, since he knew she'd be interested, to divulge at last the details concerning the several women he'd been with since their marriage seven years earlier. And it would be cheaper than a foreign film, he reasoned, or a therapist, if perhaps more costly down the stretch. But what the hey, Boccaccio.

She smiled, delighted and apprehensive, and gave him her complete attention.

"Marriage is Gondwanaland," he began, stalling, suddenly reluctant, "the human body is mostly 7-up. Between common people and heads of state there is a salty ocean. Be that as it may, here we are in bed together, can I really tell you? These past fancies were of no enduring consequence, you understand, except that they happened. Yes? Now don't get upset."

"X was a university student met on the ocean-liner to France, after you'd turned in for the evening. You were smitten with a guy from Canada, and I was feeling wounded by that, and retaliatory. A month or so later, while you were in Oxford, Carla took a train into Paris on a Saturday and we spent the night together. I remember her wide smile, and head of beautiful brown hair. She had a terrible cold, or we both did. Paris is dreary in December. I never saw her again."

"Y was an old friend from Santa Barbara, met by chance in line at a hardware store. Dancing to live music and drinking up the old familiarities did the trick. You were out of town, it was safe and sociable, really friendly. Her name was Suzanne, her young son's name was Jud. Years earlier we'd all lived in a commune in the foothills, surrounded by bamboo and walnut groves. Her ex-husband was

72

crazy, told us he'd been in the saucer with the saucer people, a real casualty. Suzanne'd taught me a few lessons back then about self-loathing, about learning to like the things I made because I made them. And that night, spent, and still excited, unable to fall asleep, I left her bed at three in the morning."

"Z was summer luck, a cute Italian traveling with a group of friends through California, a one night only vanity shot, in a lightweight leather jacket, sharing an armchair at a poetry reading, cotton t-shirt, from Bologna, we smoked weed, read Italian poets, had a ball. Claudia."

You want me to go on? You're so quiet. Were you listening? You're not upset, are you? Hey, is everything alright?

THE LINE

THE LINE "EACH TIME MY HEART is broken it makes me feel more adventurous," propels my walk to 59th & Fifth to buy a chemistry set for Clovis, before meeting Larry Fagin to preview at the Preview Theatre Richie Lerner's movie, "What Happened to Kerouac," the viewing room up narrow hallway fourth floor privacy between 48th & 49th on Broadway, on the way to which I pass Bergdorf Goodman's windows featuring quietly lit clumped dummies wearing identical Three Stooge black Moe hairpieces above Morandi-esque beige and black outfits establishing harmonies of restrained leggy color while next door the manikins spaced widely apart are wearing tuxedos, males sans features in blackface with hairless heads.

Picking dry spots on the sidewalk to place once-white tennis shoes in the post-drizzle skip across the street honking bus and braking silver limo to another set of buildings I go up five flights, up nine, up eleven, even the 12th floor has photographs and publications to scan at the elevator all cover art leaning attractively in glassed-in cases. "Give me one Glen Baxter calendar for Susan and Clark's 1986, please" with just time enough to buy a Pepsi before sitting in the dark of the theatre as the image comes up Corso teasing the interviewer with wily questioning of Kerouac's divinity. "The immortality shot?" he jabs, cocking an eyebrow, "That's a big one."

Then Ginsberg compares Jack's alcoholic suicide to a saint's mortification of the flesh.

"That's what friends are for."

Ah Manhattan flatland, all feet forward past diamonds and delis the images don't line up while the voice-over sings twilight is the loneliest time with neon buzzing where are all the coffee shops this little hole in the wall we sit in has only two chairs and there's a throng going by we don't see the tea and coffee arrive we're talking nonstop the yarns are spun of disappointment and desire, something serious, something automatic, they'd be fools to turn it down, there's a list of reprints, a Godard interview to pirate, backers to find for a one of a kind, just the right person in charge. Then we're walking past Times Square saying so long at 34th Street. Larry's got dinner plans the weather's warm but something he said makes me curious to see Bill Rice's "fey black" work so I scoot purposefully to the Patrick Fox Gallery on Bleecker minutes before closing time to assess paintings I can barely see.

I remember when the word "hair" meant balls. Surfers used it to refer to guys who'd take off on steep waves. "Fool's got hair," they'd say, with admiration, back before those balls were to the wall as "The Dirty Dozen" or "Dirty Hairy" or the Dirt Band stormed the citadel of pop history.

Annabel's key fits in the lock, Nevada the orange cat is waiting by the door, hungry. Time to rest for fifteen minutes wondering what the surface of a Duncan Hannah painting really looks like when not reduced to the size of a postcard, knowing I'll find out soon enough along with several other answers which will make up the story of my exile on Mott Street.

I say goodbye to Nevada, turn down Mott, cross Canal, stroll past Pearl Paint's racks of colored pencils, numb to the harsh grind of trucks and buses, making my way to Mel & Lizbeth's on Franklin for a dinner of lemon chicken and nourishing talk.

(NOVEMBER 14, 1985)

BUS STOP

IT'S AFTER FIVE, a black maid rides the bus down Central Avenue, asleep in her white uniform. Nothing about the smell of busses has changed since we were kids in Jr. High. Once we got off and crept close to a white woman passed out in the hibiscus lining the boulevard. What if she's dead, we worried? An empty bottle of port lay a few feet from her outstretched hand.

Then she woke, lifted her head a few inches, eyed us staring at her, growled, and fell back to sleep.

It was weirder than social studies, but not as benign as the Zoo which was adjacent and had the smell of camels munching hay as we played football in gray shorts.

Standing on the median, watching traffic go by, I wonder if the woman in white will wake at her stop. I know she's a daughter, I wonder if she's a mother. How will she endure the drudgery of another day cleaning.

I remember the hoods in their Sir Guy shirts and snap button jackets roughing up myopic innocents in the alleys walking home from school. And other tough kids who extorted lunch money from weaker ones.

Would it give me pleasure to know that those teen thugs were now humping hod for some mean contractor in a run-down C Zone, bruising their fists on the brick? Or in some other harsh way paying for their cruelty?

Tell me, jukebox, the location of that sleeping lady's stop.

PROGRAM NOTES

LEAVES HAVE FALLEN from the persimmon tree but the persimmons are still there. Hedge balls on that same Sonoma road, and camphor trees at home. The very lack of completeness, the untidiness attracts me. Detach the fig; there must be no acting. Ponderous the crude machinery of the proscenium. He stands gawking at the achievement of the boulders in the park. Full moon lavender at the line the hills make against the pale blue of dusk. I walk ahead, feeling brutal, are you one of them? World in sieve of successive words? Say more, equally slippery. Watch wheels swim backwards up Rivers of Babylon. The note quality of the syllable, hearing Elvis Costello sing "Everything means less than zero," as Ev-ry-thing descends the scale. Melody. *On parle pas comme ça.* The danger on the rocks is surely past, still I remain tied to the mast of interpretation. Thinking for five minutes in the morning, then coffee steals the day as spider monkeys swing through cages of polished bamboo in the rubble of my launch. Paragraph. It was late, I was tired, in the rain. It was my cat, lost on Potrero Hill. I stopped the car, got out, yelled "It, It, It." Under an umbrella of yellow streetlight, I was getting soaked, and then, out of nowhere, It meowed, was at my pants-cuff, make me happy! The Nova Scotia School of *Dasein*! Impulse buyers understand "crucifixation" and "pyramidriff." Ballplayers know bush league and unified infield. Three year olds grasp push for coin and every day. Stop. This won't hurt, did it? Laura discussing question marks with Steve. How much it means to the camellia tree when we laugh together. Yet when the least puff of wind would blow everything over, flecks of clairvoyance say, "pull weeds." Write what comes to light, of a knife without a blade whose handle's lost. Look up *love* in a French dictionary and find that it means bar of soap. That horrible sensation when you recommend a piece of music and someone clobbers it! Like vodka yogurt at a party you weren't invited to, one is a detail of the other. She ate two bowls, he four, watching "Once is Not Enough," on channel five, or four. This is my rosary, I'm counting on you. But for the real frijoles, turn to Book 4, Part 1 of Hume's *Treatise of Human Nature*. He had a name like Incarnadine, and he must have grown two inches during the four months he was locked up at Juvenile Hall. When you go out on a date, keep it secret, even if eventually you'll be getting out of a car and they'll see you. Interview. You've been back in Paris about a year and a half now: how does it feel? I've been watching so much TV I can't remember what it looks like. Alcohol enslaves, true? Serves as escape, false? It is worse to run out of gas with people you've just met. In the Middle East pathologists run into difficulties because religion opposes the use of Adidas on cadavers. Below is a floor plan of the plane you are in. United. I can see all that horizon, I can see it and I think I want it. But not before I look up "reify" again in Webster's Third. Segue. My chair is blue. Whoever has the dominant ear at the time. The flag of art waves over the Stygian waters, if we live to tell the story. Mail delivery by dugout canoe is iffy. To suggest we disappear in concentrated effort is to "see" the impossible realized. I am hostile, aggressive, contemptuous; I got here by automobile. There must be no acting. Persimmons. United.

(NOVEMBER 26, 1977)

UP
THE WAZOO

For my god-daughters
Nadia Szold and Bridget Mendel

THE REWARD

James Siena pays the greatest
possible attention

to something
whose importance

he knows is a measure
of its reality to him.

The line—his line readings,
his magnetic hums—echoes

in the optic nerve. Not velocity,
this line: it's all going

nowhere fast, as direction,
weaving through traffic

on a ten speed, Mets on
radio, cell phone ringing,

sausage in a string bag,
decision's daily knife.

And if edge is shape,
figure ground,

matter atmosphere?
Procedures nest

in heartless logic.
Contour shaves necessity.

His widths declare existence
seamless and factual.

No Atlas of brazen format,
his algorithms play "Taps"

with bugle energy, play
"Embraceable You" on a ukulele

to stay true. At the end of
the day, by dawn's early light,

you see what's there by looking
(take the hit, note the rigor,

feel the stamina, yield to
perception's human reach)

selfless as a peach.
The reward is to be a source.

RENE RICARD NIGHT AT BILL BERKSON'S FRANK O'HARA TALK AT POETS HOUSE ON SPRING STREET

"Imagine admirers carrying tiny Alexander Pope around
on pillows," Rene said. "Think of Lautrec," I said. "Yes,"
Rene adds, "he was even smaller. People called him 'the teapot'
because he was hung like one. I sold a painting
this morning for $30,000. I don't have to write
about art, I just pick the best works. I'm going to see
Clemente on Thursday, he'll do my tenth portrait.
You visit me at the Chelsea, don't mention your name
or my name, just the room number. Guys I don't
even know come along and jackoff on my door!"

Then Rene leans in conspiratorially, says this or that
in gasping tones while eating grapes and cheese-sticks
non-stop, looking trim with short stubble and hat
and glamorous shades hiding his eyes, P-coat buttoned
his body non-stop buzzing movement back and forth,
side to side, what's fueling this movement?
When I mention that years ago E. had told me
he was sick, Rene straightens up, says, "I've never
been sick a day in my life, never even had VD.
She doesn't know me, she never knew me!"

(Instantly wished I hadn't mentioned her name.)
Mollify, mollify. Brings up the fire in his apartment,
that he lost everything, that the extent of the other
tenants' sympathy was, "The spines of my books got wet!"

"And I lost everything!" he moans. Later, S. tells me
Rene started the fire, never called the fire department,
and fled! In the Chelsea now he gets calls for
interviews all the time, never keeps anything. Gives
everything away: books, drawings, prints, things.
Tells me Brice picked him up at 9:15 this morning

for a private viewing of the Marden show at MOMA.
"In the late pictures his light is positively Venetian,
his studio's on the Hudson, the late stuff is rich,
I won't tell you! Scrubbed color, as if the light were
bouncing up from the water, as well as coming in on
the air." Then the reception ended. Rene and
Raymond dissolved into the night. And I remember
wondering, if on their way down, Rene would have
asked Raymond who that guy was he was talking to?
Or if by the time they hit the street it would even matter?

(NOVEMBER 28, 2006)

THE MADNESS OF DAWN

I am irritably reaching
I can not get through on the phone
I have stayed in one place with a roof over my head

I am asking for light
I am exposed from head to foot
I am utterly alone and quizzical

I am the plaything of an immortal delirium
I think I picked up my appearance in the street
I am a bag of water

I lean against the outer wall
I am reduced to shallow breathing
I nearly lose my sight

I am face to face with the madness of dawn
I want to see it in full sunlight
I want to invent a winning stratagem

I am carrying everything on my back
I am plagued by unjust thoughts
I will rid myself of myself

I will tell you the whole story
I am the one who needs it
I am not the kind of man who is satisfied with words

HAIL AND FAREWELL

Counting eight spokes in each Piero Della Francesca wheel
I leave motion to the Futurists, bad dreams in a notebook.
It's easier to listen with a mouthful of food.
No, I'm not sitting on a ukulele. I know how to make
This scene play "Chopsticks." But that's not why
My Romanticism's on a bender. I'm just
Coleridgean enough to put off the perceived

Consequences of any thought, including "Behold this fleeting
World how all things fade." Be gone, sad bio-pics.
Turning sixty I'm thinking that that
Which has not killed me yet has made me strong,
Then I vow to swear off the platitudes and boil the rice.
So many soldiers, so few battles, so many trumpets,
So few horns. "Flying is such a great way to get somewhere,

Too bad there's no place to go," said the critic,
While my eyes raked the Ligurian coast.
Sometimes we must deliver a crushing blow to a friend,
Especially one running on nothing stronger than
Subsistence dabbling (doing just enough work to
Entertain an ego, but not a soul). Without a song, where
Are you? Art's fine line excites the mind.

KATHLEEN

A.
I can't read the books.
I can't even read reviews of the books.
I've stopped going to movies, stopped eating fast food.
I feel a knot in my stomach watching the Mets on TV.
I keep thinking of her.
She is the right height, the right complexion.
She is the right shape, the right size.
She has lips that stretch like taffy when she smiles.
Her humor tickles me.
She makes listening easy when she talks.
She makes me feel strong feelings when we touch.
She furrows her brows in thought like Jack Nicholson.
Her arms cannot be described, they are so perfect
And the bones in her wrists a delicate crime.
There is a mystery at the core of her being.
I am outside that core, surveying its veils.
And to think that six months ago I didn't know her.
To think that six months ago I was alone.
With a fast mind, a blue eye, and an ear for idioms
She says she must go deep within herself.
She must clear a space, a time, and a place in which to work.
I want to say what her ambition means to me.

B.
She warms whole milk for morning coffee.
She spreads raspberry jam on breakfast toast
And with fingers picks up a fat chunk of canteloupe.

She lifts a fork with her left hand.
She sets a timer when steaming vegetables.
She values a good salad.
She is incorruptibly fair-minded, generous and open.
She takes the subway, but will use a car service.
She shares, then disappears, in order to work.
She writes on lined tablets,
Types her work into a blue laptop.
Is she patient? Is she willful? Is she acting?
She returns calls, later.
I admire her. But I don't know her.
She can act silly on a tennis court, but keep the point alive.
She knows the city, on foot, by subway, or car.
She's been at it a long time
Yet strolls up the street like a kid newly minted.
She lies on her tummy.
She gasps a little when turned on
Face flushed with sinuous feeling.
She sleeps with mouth closed under a light blanket.
She wakes in good spirits after scribbling a dream.
She says she is difficult.
I am beginning to understand her.
The paper is delivered to her door.
She says she needs to earn more money.
She walks the bag of laundry to the cleaners.
She is proud of, she is attentive to,
She organizes her daughters
Who shower her with hugs, kisses and teenage "duh" looks.
She hears their concerts, knows where they are,
Makes sure they're safe.

I would let her hold a knife to my throat.
I would vote for her to lead a cause.
She responds to new people immediately
But is devoted to old friends.
By day she prefers to write a play
Or go to a theatre box-office for tickets.
At night if it's right she might sip whiskey.
Good with British accents, good with Beach Boys songs,
She cocks an ear as her daughters practice violins.
She has a favorite player on a favorite baseball team
She falls asleep on a sofa watching.
She falls prey to doubt, asks herself why.
She trusts her therapist.
She wants to be free but she's not sure of what.
The key word is focus, she must bear down, go deep.
In close she likes honest talk, genuine affection.
Soft hands, true tongue, mutual satisfaction.

C.
She feels suffocated in relationships.
From too much social life she needs to retreat.
She ends our affair, with a phone call.
She stays home quietly, gathering her strength.
She pays bills, calls for messages, straightens up.
She runs with a friend on Saturday mornings.
I've written this about her and now she's gone.
I don't know why she didn't let me have it.
I don't know why she weeded me from Eden.
I do know she had me fooled at times.
Nine months is a birth, even stillborn.

Took me in a daughter's room to watch the sweet heart sleep.
Got me on the sofa and kissed me passionately.
Weekends of pleasure, talk, activity,
But some things ain't meant to be.
Always some resistance, some doubtful edge.
A reluctance to fit herself to another.
What causes the game to change, the other to be diminished?
Now I've more time, and more questions.
Now I'm focussed on my work.
Now I'm not vulnerable to her moods.
Now I'm getting some distance.
Now I'm checking things off the list.
Soon I'll return her few items.
Soon I'll pick up my few things.
Soon it will be more than over.
Soon the magic will be memory.
Soon the seasons will intervene.
Soon the moon will be new.

HEART OF THE BREATH

"They know I'm here, but do I?"
Jim Brodey

Thank you Jim, for another rich hour of compressed
gas, manic precision and weed-lot genius. I'm dedicating
this morning's orange glow to your vast amalgams,
catching you in the company of souls that watered your desert,
junked your streets, and prized your debris. I'll never

forget the letter you wrote me when I didn't accept a five
page poem you'd submitted to an issue of Stooge in 1974.
You tore me up, gleefully working your righteous indignation
into humorous assault. That letter, like your life, is gone now,
along with everything back then, boxes tossed by an angry

mother-in-law. A million years later I met you at the
Telephone Bar after Clark had read at the Church
and I wondered as we shook hands, if you'd remembered writing
it, that I was the same guy who'd sent your poem back to you,
unloved. I registered your sly smile but didn't bring it up.

Wish I had them now to reread, both poem and letter.
Clark edited your *Heart* with great respect for its energy &
feeling, guided by brotherly affection in the retyping and
ordering of your relentless sprawl and curiously intimidating
stamina, to make sure your life's devotion to poetry not be lost.

ON THE OAT TOUR

People who deceive us
by wearing normal faces
are a bear to identify; we must
remain vigilant in the presence

of stylists and beauticians
lest they catch fire as we drive by.
Things that are the property
of the very few are not for us.

Each touch of the garrulous
is a medieval façade.
May I bum your machine to make
fake rain fall on curb light?

Only gargoyles fear the sudden
climbing of summer hollyhocks.
Let me secure this camera on a tripod.
I must be rebuilt as a dark house,

quick enough to give evening some lip.
Please drop your codex in my box.
All I can smell here is newsprint
and indifference nibbling peach halves.

Pixies are good at removing the weight
of laurels from restive giants.
You can hire a taxi to air out
your found mattress,

But never acknowledge a holiday.
Distance is intimacy. Banquo stalks
the mall where hungry ghosts
toy with dressing younger.

Is there really only one thing
that can destroy us? Huddled
under a sheet in the fetal position?
What can we do for people who are not

here yet? Say, three centuries hence?
Write at night with an oar on water?
Drop through a funnel that gives
these words lonesomeness?

We are but one in a billion pulses
reveling in phone culture as fog-horns
sound the arrival of trickster oceans.
I like this house because it's yours.

GOT

Got by a player in straight sets yesterday
Which is, quite simply, and in four words, why I was born,
By workmanlike attention to the corners.
Now it's Sunday, the day of rest, a wholly fictional device.
I feel disobediently Miltonic and Methodist.
I'm one with my character now: nasty, cold-blooded, febrile.
My canoe is untethered, my banjo unstrung. Could be
A woman brings me luck, could be dim sum.

I might take a bike ride somewhere soon,
Maybe look you up on the way. Jerk us up
A couple of sodas with some kind of deadly drug
In them? I know I could be a great ellipsis.
I'm watching the bug of time crawl down my lifeline
With its stinger unsheathed toward that railroad crossing
With Fate. Looks like it might be a tasty accident.
But you know all shut eyes ain't sleep
And all goodbyes ain't gone. Write me a note,

Buy me a bottle. I'll go ahead and debone this
Chicken any way you'll read me. Everything's too quiet
Here at the Villa Cilantro. Gray matter stretched
From ear to ear. A vernal equinox of the soul. Seems
My brain is in the hands of the Crime Lab Division, anyway.
Don't mention this to what's her name, though, or
I'll have to bump you off. You know too much, see?
God is a concept, by which we censure our gain.

THE 97TH KENTUCKY DERBY

She yelled
the horses are prancing through introductions
& I dropped the book of *Job*
hustled in
& heard we had six minutes til post-time.
She'd just put on short pants and a shirt
after taking a bath & was trying
to get a comb through her long tangled hair.

I said wait a minute
unsnapped her pants
pulled them down around her thighs
slid down her standing body
& buried my tongue in her moist bush.
I perfumed it, she said.
I can taste it, I said.

Pretty soon I was sitting on the floor
& she was sitting on me
riding me back and forth
yelling giddiup giddiup
way out ahead of those other horses
who hadn't even arrived at the starting gate yet.
I heard a trumpet announce something & the crowd got excited

& carefully I manoeuvered her until she was flat
on her back, head below the TV
and now I was riding her, rocking gently

not even racing now
as the announcer spoke of the Derby's glorious history.

Arching her back, she looked upside down
at the horses on the screen
some in the starting gate
others glistening and edgy and powerful
about to enter
but we couldn't wait for them
& in a beautiful homestretch
at least a minute before Cañonero II
won the 97th Kentucky Derby by three lengths
we kicked it all the way home.

WHAT'S IN STORE

The speaking body knows
The operation of thought
Requires nervous energy in the brain

But what does this herald on a Wednesday morning?
The first of February 1978 with Paul
And little Daniel still sleeping upstairs

And Lydia holed up in Clovie's room writing
Something to be read here Friday night
And Laura just showered emerging

In brown French worker's overalls
And Clayton about to arrive on BART for lunch?
"Praising thy works continually with song

As mortals should," is the answer provided
By Cleanthes' "Hymn to Zeus"
While I play Jackie McLean & Dexter Gordon

Dilating upon a theme from Grofe, of all the crazy.
Will we get a sandwich at Walnut Square
Or hold out for Chez Panisse & cold Sancerre?

Grizley Peak sits atop Grizley Peak
The way Jackie's alto paints rivers of tin
Flowing down Cedar Street in a tailspin.

ON THE LIZ WILLIS AVENUE BRIDGE

My fellow virgins, my boy comets, my burning suns . . .
If you survive Spring's background check
Writing at tables with gryphon feet
It will take practice to state the obvious
It will take galoshes to walk through Venice.

Dear Impermanence, may I measure your lashes?
I want to be alone with you.
My balloons will aspirate your flesh.
Our best and brightest goats will chew on your hem at Dawn

While your "*je*" navigates a boiling sea under some "*autre*" sky
With only a floor fan to cool its apostasy.
Can we hire Artemis to make sense
Of a gull's love of garbage? Sign Ariadne to free our hands
From the ivy that spells "only connect?"

Let me squint at your white-washed village, Evangelia,
Hang a laurel wreath on the screen door of Plato's Cave.
We predict gulf storms; we don't prepare for them.
Heroes stomp wineskins with iambic feet.

Self-rule explodes in bottles of hair.
Who will rinse the grime from the eyes of auto-didacts?
Who can forgive Texas its lethal applesauce?
American soil is blowing in the air.
Tires hiss over the grillwork of this bridge.

UP THE WAZOO

I see your dreams and a strange fog in the trees.
If my body's not there at spring's debut, I know
your soul's dazzling rain will nourish the flowers.
In this late light my beard is white, and all things,
even the red owl and the parked car, shiver. The path
disappears. The path has fallen asleep. Remember me?
I would wake up wind-tanned and florid, to watch you
fill with crystal light. Lovely for weeping, tinged
for flight. A drum pounds the night long, the thud
of the dead unlocking our door. Can I be a white
mule ornamented with grief? I am ruined.

Was it a joke, our palm of thrashing fronds?
You were my demented Queen among birches.
Silence is old hat, rival archer of those who have
given their eyes to the sky. Gardens hold love
for seasons, heads open like lilies. Some day
we'll die for love, oh yes! without once looking back.
Paint me again, even badly, that I may seem unreal.
Starlings sweep the skies, drenching the road
in shadow. Remembrance, the blind bee of
bitterness, why be haughty and brief? Why fight
off this ardent burgeoning?

The cradle of dreams is rocked by boredom
repeated in the stream of everything withdrawing
into soul. What is above, unperturbed,

if not the breeze, reminding us to love the dark!
Like an immaculate sword, a strange
emptiness glints when I see you in the clear.
Already of deep promise, shall I count your
treasures? Comes a voice, reaching the senses
through flesh. Soul is sated with body's gold!
Writing adds heat to the cold, as illness murders
the breeze. The soul's not a color to be attained.
Happiness falls slowly, shatters if false. The true

guardian of a life lived connects slow heart
beats to a sky hard and white. Now
we are nothing but the roots of dahlias. Today
I gaze at you lingeringly, brimming over with
the immense plenitude of gateways leading here.
How strange we are with our earth-born feet,
quiet and complete as joy when meaning
ceases. I know that when the ax of dawn lights
the slippery dunes, you will continue to watch me
though I be hushed in shadow. Threads bind us
to what is absent. We want to be together.

A book is a canteen filled with solitude, a
butterfly of light articulating the sorrow of life.
Enter the depths with something of open measure
beginning once again along the path, asking of
love and laughter, "what do you see?"
The crimson zenith is covered with old newspapers
propelled by human will, the water of simple sight.
To empty oneself completely! Mine of sublime

secrecy. I am the black dummy on your lap
whose voice is language. Look a little, endless
sun. Vain explosions light up inward skies

with colors to dress a restive species,
a timeless vase, a pomegranate, a figure-eight.
The present starts yesterday, parallel to our sleep,
this not knowing our own death, the real silver
drops on petals. Close the door the way she likes it.
And like a palm tree draped with fire opals,
our shadows enlarge, fill out, entwine, flee to limit
the blue, sole wave without break. The star
in your eyes evaporates as charity flies.
Death is a king's pigeon. I want to reach the shore,
this infinity that language yearns for! Let nothing

invade me from without, nor bite without lips.
The thorn is here to kindle a sharp cry above the stone
of the world. I have only the fountain of today, this
mad murmur of all murmurs, alert, self-possessed,
a halo, an aura of white fire limning the roadways
to be the you you long to be among so many heads,
so many breasts, this certainty that absorbs us
and looks at signal night as if rocked in the
fulfillment of last consciousness, green sea, blue dawn
the image of my faith in your beauty, moments when
hand or kiss or glance makes the skin of time glow.

RON PADGETT READS AT LOCUS MEDIA, 594 BROADWAY, NOV. 30, 2000, 6:30–8:30 PM

"Okie synesthesia," he says, "features riot cloth
wiping hapless mildew away," then clears his throat
of chaste bio-rhythms to speak of "the author."
But there is nothing in that drawer. Anti-sonnets,
as in, "who lacks for grasshoppers restlessly waves
off a sandwich," masquerade as *hors d'oeuvres*
                    before our hero of lined foolscap scissors *semes*
to the floor--the floor of mental illness, mind you--
touching things no finger on a raw-boned hand should touch.
Like hip replacement, movement is character. Praying
is begging. Things mean what they say. Poetry paws
through a pile of trash bags obscuring a hydrant.
                    This is one fella who truly needs a fiery sunset
painted with Huntz Hall's brains. There's an evolutionary
reason for the lack of green hair. Each generational torso
is attached to basic limbs. I must scale this
Louisiana perch, he says. I've got a hunch some hooks
are cognate with flare-ups of endometriosis.
                    If this poem's out of order, call the line
doctor. No cell service? Take a moment to cut up
Gravity's Rainbow. We're losing altitude, faking attitude.
There's frost on the keys, a heap of rust on sad fleets
churning off to war. To the sleeping lion St. Jerome says,
"It's the triangle offense, stupid."
                    A light year later a manicured hand paints
a beach ball around The Donald's waist, but Lorca
only *proposed* that his racquet be restrung

by a passing cloud. Should night open its motel door
to the Delphic chimp? Free agents dip their ladles
into the cauldron of roadside deities
                    that the day's somersaults not upend us
nor the muzzle of a dog's rough charm shake our pantheism.
Troubling questions require more pillow than the Brahms
lullaby. In packed coffeehouses nicotine from
centuries ago stains *The Euphues*. I've been meaning
to say something to the Countess of Pembroke
                    about Sidney's courtly shamanism: "As rhetoric
goes, so goes Stella's *ars poetica*." When the author
peers inside his strophe he sees a Winkfield pineapple
set upon by wasps. When I peer into the empty Davis Cup
of what is happening to the finesse game, I see raw
power smacking scuds to every corner.
                    Will the author ever know that I am here?
He defends his farmer's daughter from messianic
woodpeckers, that her heart be safe with him.
But let me give her nightly rant a backrub. I miss
the way she praises a comma. And I miss the way
we used to talk in our cots in the dark.
                    Ah, to know a wink from *un clin d'oeil!*
I like hearing his feet shuffle on old floorboards,
calling through river fog: "Jimmy, *dis-moi*, if you're
out there, crying in the fragile hamburger, is it true
that babies born into misery register every detail
till the milk dries up?" *Bonjour tristesse. Au revoir.*

CAN'T GET NO WHOLE ONE BLUES

Why should anything any one
    keep on going if not
        ever at any time anything
any one will be a whole one,
    what is the use of anything
        or everything keeping on
going if not at any time
    I will not be having
        a sensation that any one
anything will be a whole one,
    once every one sometime was
        a whole one, now mostly

every one is a piece of a one,
    not all the being
        as a complete one and yet
every one has their own being
    in them and putting all of each
        kind of them together
to make a whole one can
    not be to me a satisfaction
        cannot give to me any real
satisfaction can not be a
    satisfactory way in my feeling
        of having completion of

having anything or any one a whole
    one cannot give to me any reason

why the world should keep
on being, there is not any reason
  if in repeating nothing
    is giving to me a
sensation of a completed one,
  I have then this in me
    now and mostly
every one I am
  knowing or remembering
    is to me just

now a piece of a kind
  of being and every one
    is themselves inside them,
that is always to my
  feeling certain and so then
    feeling each one is
a piece of a kind
  of being and always then
    feeling each one is
entirely existing so that
  each one is not a part of any
    whole thing I cannot to myself

have any very real satisfaction
  from getting together
    all the ones there are
of a kind of them,
  to make a whole one,
    that is, not to my feeling,

that cannot give to me an emotion
    of satisfaction, that is not
        to my feeling satisfying
and so then I am not feeling
    each one is sometime to me
        a whole one, no then no,

I am now feeling that mostly
    all of them every one
        I am knowing I am
remembering is to me a piece
    of being and so then
        there is not any use
in the world going on
    existing so that every one
        can keep on with repeating
a piece of being, not any use
    at all then to me to my feeling
        not any use then really to any one

and this is now then the real
    state of feeling
        I am now having.